Left Hand

Elizz Correa

Presentation by *BookLeaf Publishing*

Web: www.bookleafpub.com

E-mail: info@bookleafpub.com

ISBN: 9789357442053

First edition 2023

DEDICATION

My mom,

"Where did you come from?"

ACKNOWLEDGEMENT

Thank you Roswell, Georgia for the amour to learn from what's past and cry until you're ready again.

PREFACE

This is a root of stories I stopped thinking about so frantically a few years into psychotherapy. The paragraphs are excerpts from climbed stairs and always choosing both the ups and the downs. I cnoose to grow alone and think holistically. The writing closes a gap so gray I had to learn how to climb with purpose and hope and pray God was at the top or bottom of these stages of life. There's a page on realizing there's no return and that everything's leading to figuring it out on my own without someone stopping to ask how I am on the clock at work. There's a passage about walking and about smoking and about the Grand Budapest Hotel. Drink tea like I learned to and remember the sharper side of knowledge while you read so it doesn't hurt while you read like I did writing it and instead grows love

Georgia, you're crying

let's say i move to New York and get a job for
artmajeur.com and i take a sip of coffee and the
caffeine didn't explode but soothed and going
outside was going on stage except i'm a blurb
and the script is already written and when the
gallery art feels like the page i read before
climbing out of my top bunk i feel i aced the
homework i gave myself

I feel...

I taught myself a lesson on letting go last night. I quit my side jobs to have a little brain power for what I love and maybe I could ask God to help me grow there. There's a control I felt when I was reaching 20 years old that I otherwise wouldn't have felt ever again. Maybe not for years. I'm still battling my illnesses and I think they're going to send me home.

Home

3

Sometimes I call home and regret it immediately. I think it's chaos well-traveled and coming forwards in time to smite me. Each raised eyebrow after the fact is a solemn gesture made by it to me for recognition of... 'let's see what it is today'... "do you know how much that costs?" or "I told you so" after a dilemma so private exposes itself on to the sidewalk like ashes and I quite actually raise my left eyebrow out of disgust for the whole thing ever finding a warm spot in my stomach- for even giving it attention that belongs to something else

My love

my love is a puppy
 my love is flowers
  my love is good
circle me in warmth
please make them polite
have them open the door
  remind me my past is conquerorable
   say you like it when we both know you do
    look close but away when i smile for him
my love is there and that and this
my love tricks me out
my love touchs me
  when i party hand me favors i'll do them
   if i say no i secretly meant yes
My love is baby and mom and "please go first."
Picture me beside you and picture me naked I'm
sure you've done both.

Free

On my walk today I snapped a photo of
drawings of faces on printer paper taped to an
electricity box on the lower Westside.
I had an epiphany that you and her and me
turned out okay.
I always looked misplaced those years and
hopefully after and you always had your smart
thing going on and she looked right through and
didn't buy a thing and we loved her for that.
As I had this epiphany, hoping I could get to
work and find something valuable for my
submissions, I saw myself in the reflection of
my glasses dividing into the three of us and the
ones who took care of us and how much love we
had and how my mind couldn't explain it

I Love You, I Love You, I Do

i am remembering
i am taking out the bad by sourcing
i am sound and medicating
i am balancing

afterlife

I don't Go to concerts anymore. The kind of scene where I felt as famous and important as the artists set to seem like they're skateboarding down Ponce de Leon Avenue even after the show. I had a feeling those questions were for eons from that spot on the concrete where guidance shown through education of sitting on the ground waiting for sets like going in for a soccer game. Questions like who and what and where and why all in someone's cigarette out of line and patient. I wish you'd seen it I say to the God and I laugh because he brought me there.

Don't curse

My body doesn't sing how it used to. I have a researchable body now. The hospitals and clinics fascinate me and I wonder how the pain will stop if I don't remember the first time. I want nothing more than the delight of being able to solve my changes in youth and my healing to measure to the pain.

Healing

I hope I don't knock the daylights out of myself too much more. I'm writing to you past and we both know I meant to contact the present. If things smooth over there's a passageway I hope I can get to in time.

Tumblr

Scroll through Tumblr and read about all the
drama in the history of drama and come back to
life. Watch a lesbian porno again after liking it
the first time. Say nothing about that but come to
class with your eyes blotched from crying a
good nights 2-hour sleep. That was teens.

Cure

I think I'm awakening here in New York. I want nicer days. I want easier days. I left my days of heartsickeness behind if I will. I want nothing hard. I want nothing mean.

humans

us human with our gunks and our smells
us humans with our mistreatments and
misjudgments
us humans with our bruises and our funks
us humans with our callouses and bleeding
us humans with our pining and our grasping
us humans with our funks

Proud

I had a nightmare last night about you know
who. That last day of school when we unpacked
our backpacks and left to play outside I laughed.
The stacks we meant to burn in the fireplace
reappeared after the accident. I got my dress
dirty and when I came home I burned it in the
fire. The same one from the photo in the
yearbook congratulating us for our style. Don't
tell me I'm crazy for doing all that. Don't tell me
I was stupid or nonchalant. I think I should've
used a thesaurus as a pillow after that.

Grandpa

Tell me tall tales. Don't wait until the end. Show me love in all its places and come back in black and blue and khaki. Open up tents and show me The Royal Tenenbaums before clicking out of 'Queen Bitch.' Send me stars and feather me in princess wands. Hold my bow freely and Georgia smile. Grandpa come back and hold Marta's hand and whisper in her ear so I can know. Chew corn and stop eating bread so I can know. Wear sandals while walking the dog and print out photos of us in the dining room staring at photos of space and The Velvet Underground album cover in the candlelight. Let's do it again every week but fly me to Mars for the holidays.

Fear

send me a stream of music from my periods
cross me with vocals steep and belly
just find me a degree
send all the dead out of me so I can see
Torture me with goodness
desire my flow of lace
oh please bring me back!

Universidad

i want want one for happiness
one for undereating
one for killing time
one for children's teeth
one for never stepping on cracks in the sidewalk
one for saying thank you and sorry
one for kindness
one for warm colors
and one for loops and hoops

changes

You're so groovy.
Hold me.

Marina Keegan

Looking through windows.

I'm sorry if I missed you.

I was left behind.

I wanted to give you oral pleasure.

"Let's start a band" - I ask in the Navy sorta type

In a safe place ofcourse

Did I break the rules?

2.

'"Let's start a band" - I ask in the Navy'

Looking through windows.

I'm sorry if I missed you.

I was left behind.

I wanted to give you oral pleasure.

In a safe place ofcourse

Did I break the rules?

3.

Looking through windows high on the MTA.

I'm sorry if I missed you it was on...

I was left behind you whisper.

I wanted to give you oral pleasure.
SERIOUSLY

"Let's start a band" - he asks in the Navy

In a safe place ofcourse.

Did I break the rules *.*.(it's broken).*.* I mean
can you play the piano while I sing Art?! Or else
I might have to go to the park.

Pillows

I remember my mother setting the table.
The bowl of piegeon pea soup, the spoon, and a
paper towel, over the placemat that's over a
towel.

five

I brushed my early 20s while Supersymmetry by Arcade Fire dozed off in the background. I didn't brush my teeth or use soap I'd just sit under the showerhead in 'Christian camps' in Chinatown. By November I was sick of the winter. I'd leave, I'd come back, I'd leave I'd come back like swings. Tears flowed from my eyes in advance and from the cellars of wine on my first trip living in a home recognized by witchcraft. I'm new to this social thing and I'm not used to it. I got myself a present for that future but as of now I'm unable to tell when it's coming. Come faster. Come freely. Come ambushed and sore. Lay your head on my head while my heart talks over the medicine prescribed. We, remember we strictly we.

God

Florence and the Machine me to Mars to visit Grandpa.